THREAT INTELLIGENCE and ME

A Book for Children and Analysts

by
Robert M. Lee

Illustrated by
Jeff Haas

ISBN-13: 978-1541148819
ISBN-10: 1541148819

Printed in the United States

Robert M. Lee is is the CEO and Founder of the industrial cyber security company Dragos, Inc. He is also a non-resident National Cybersecurity Fellow at New America focusing on policy issues relating to the cyber security of critical infrastructure. For his research and focus areas, Robert was named one of Passcode's Influencers, awarded EnergySec's Cyber Security Professional of the Year (2015), and inducted into Forbes' 30 under 30 for Enterprise Technology (2016).

A passionate educator, Robert is the course author of SANS ICS515 – "Active Defense and Incident Response" and the lead author of SANS FOR578 – "Cyber Threat Intelligence."

Robert obtained his start in cyber security in the U.S. Air Force where he served as a Cyber Warfare Operations Officer. He has performed defense, intelligence, and attack missions in various government organizations including the establishment of a first-of-its-kind ICS/SCADA cyber threat intelligence and intrusion analysis mission. Lastly, Robert, along with Jeff Haas, creates a weekly technology and security web comic titled Little Bobby.

Jeff Haas is a wide-ranging freelance illustrator always on the lookout for exciting new projects. He collaborated with Robert on "SCADA and Me", the first Little Bobby book, in 2013 and has since translated it into Spanish, German and Japanese.

His work had been featured in a variety of theater posters, role-playing games , and news articles in The Christian Science Monitor and Quartz.

More of Jeff's work can be seen at jeffhaas.daportfolio.com

Continue the adventure with the Little Bobby weekly comic which can be found at www.LittleBobbyComic.com and on Twitter @_LittleBobby_

Made in the USA
Middletown, DE
19 January 2017